How to Win At Life by Being a Smug, Self-Righteous, Smarmy, Grinning, Self-Help Twat

By
Karl A. Mercer

How to Win At Life by Being a Smug, Self-Righteous, Smarmy, Grinning Self-Help Twat
Copyright ©Karl Anthony Mercer 2009-2011
ISBN 978-1-4710-7378-6
All rights reserved.

What follows is a work of self-righteous, opinionated fiction. If you find any similarity in characters, situations, locations, words, expressions, punctuation etc. then you probably over think things. It's not a bad trait by any means, but I am sure it sometimes gets you into trouble. But have no fear, I did not write any of this about you personally, nor am I stalking you to steal your character, situations or locations. Just relax, take a deep breath, and believe me. The author asserts the moral right under the Copyright, Designs and Patents Act 1988 to be identified as the author of this work. No part of this material may be reproduced or transmitted in any form or stored in a retrieval system without the prior written consent of the author. That means no stealing, online pirates! With your pixelated eyepatches and flash-animation parrots! Do you reckon guys in publishing or copyright who don't want kids tell their partners by saying, of themselves, "no part of this material may be reproduced"? I'd like to imagine they do.

Introduction

You know the types of books? Smarmy, grinning motherfuckers on the front covers with teeth so white they blind you with cosmetic-surgery and photoshopped brightness. These are generally 'from nothing' tales, or 'lies' as I like to call them, where someone tells you how they grew up in the middle class, suburban ghettos struggling to eat because there was not a store nearby that sold organic, gluten free, dairy free pasta and having to struggle all their lives, working their fingers to the bone grafting in such physically taxing careers as salesperson, shop owner, middle-manager, or financial services executive.

Well, this is one of those types of books! In it, I will reveal all my secrets of how I came to be a successfully unemployed mental patient. I will patronise you by telling you it is your attitude that is the problem, and that you not working hard enough! I will reveal the true secrets to success (at failure) and hopefully I shall enlighten you.

Chapter 1: It's all about your attitude!

Positivity! It is all about positivity! And not having it! You see if you're positive about things you leave no scope for negativity, something which is rife throughout the world. I know you get lots of these books by 'successful' people telling you positivity was the key to their success, but they would say that, wouldn't they? They would not want to be so humble as to concede that actually it was just blind luck! Their egos refuse to allow them to think that they just happened to be in the right place at the right time, no, they *must* have put themselves in the right place at the right time because they're successful and you're not!

I am not sure of the official current global population figures but I think now it is over seven billion. That's 7,000,000,000 – and you are one of them... That means there are over 6,999,999,999 other human individuals who want the same things you do, personal happiness and success. So why then do we put so much weight on the thoughts and attitudes of the few who happen to be lucky enough to get anywhere? If it were as easy as attitude, it is implying that the smug individuals writing these success-tip books believe themselves to be better than 6,999,999,999 other people. Now call me a cynic, but that seems pretty ridiculous and illogical to me. Do you know what does not seem illogical? They got lucky, end of story.

They'll always harp on about attitude, attitude, attitude - But what of talent? Skills? Deserving? Effort? It implies that an idiot whose very existence is merely a waste of oxygen and nutrients should be more deserving than a hard working pessimist simply because this individual believes in themselves!? I call bullshit! And pandering to this nonsense myth is only exacerbating the problem! And there's a good reason individuals with success like to promote this myth. Because people blinded by individualistic egotism and faith in themselves are easier to exploit and manipulate. Masturbation of the ego is one of the easiest ways to manipulate individuals, and those who have no ego to masturbate are impervious to such underhand tactics.

Is this not usually the part where the smug, self-righteous author puts in a personal anecdote to back up their claims? Okay, I shall play along with it. A few years ago, I got a job at an insurance company. A large company in the region, the prospects for career advancement and climbing up the payscale were fantastic, and I had other family members there to support me all the way. Sadly, the work was soulless and empty, I despised it. I despised the people I had to talk to on the telephone, and their attitudes. I despised the work ethic that seemed to essentially be 'screw the customer out of as much money as possible' and most of all, I despised the organisation itself. So what did I do? Keep my chin up? Work hard at it? Try to pull through to get a better place in the hierarchy, a company car, more responsibility and a larger wage packet? Fuck no! Don't be stupid! No amount of bullshit personal wealth, monetary success or organisational sycophantics is worth selling your soul and losing your mind over. Instead, I decided I should reassess quite what I wanted to do with my life, and ended up with a place at a very reputable university in the UK studying for a science degree and enjoying every minute of it! Negativity got me to that location! Were I a positive individual I would have stuck it out, I would have believed it was the right thing to do and all the success was what I wanted. I'd have pushed to improve my sales figures to the detriment of what customers truly needed, and I would have lost my soul in the process. Every employee of the month award would have existed purely to masturbate my ego, every commission bonus there only to fool me that this is what I wanted to be doing whilst slowly a man's soul is being eroded by banality and repetition.

Don't believe the bullshit. A positive attitude is the best way for you to be exploited and come out of a barrel of roses smelling like shit. I'm not saying be negative either. Merely be objective. If you feel positive in a situation then good for you, enjoy it. If you feel negative in a situation then do not think that is wrong. Do not believe you have no right to feel negative. Instead, set about planning to how you can change it. What changes do you need to make to your personal or professional life that can get you back to being positive? In some cases you may find the answers to be drastic, as indeed in my case where I had to leave a steady, decent paying job. But it made me happy to leave! I did not care about the money, I was working to achieve something I wanted to do and not something society expected I should do. When you sign up for a job these days and they ask for your personal goals, they don't want to hear how you aspire to write poetry for a living, or how one day you'd like to travel the Far East, or how you've always wanted to have your own ice cream shop. They do not care what you want to achieve for you, only what they want you to achieve for them! So please, maintain objectivity. If something is not going the way you expect, do not think you have to be positive and push through it, it is your right as a human being to say "fuck this!" and do something else entirely. Many people have done so, most have failed...But I bet if you asked any of them whether they regret it they could look you seriously in the eye and with a steely determination say to you "Not at all!" Because to fail means at least you had the guts to try in the first place, and that in itself is a better reward than any promotion and provides riches greater in life than any bank balance.

So attitude? Pfft...Not Important, you can stuff it. You are who you are and that should not be changed, if you are a naturally negative person just learn to make it work for you. Some people are just like that, it is no character flaw, it does not mean that there is something wrong with you. There is natural variation in all creatures and it is evident in the human attitude, and if you're a business or organisation that only wants to hire positive people then you are essentially an exploiter of other people's good natures and can go get fucked with a shovel. I would hire a miserable individual with a brain rather than a bundle of vapid positive energy any day. You ask them both what colour you should paint your bathroom walls, Captain Positive will rush off and spend hours researching the most inviting, ergonomic, economically viable, environmentally friendly paint possible. The miserable person shall say "It doesn't matter; it'll still be full of shit." Which is more sensible?

Heavenly Bodies

Looking up, naively, at the clear night sky

I see not stars twinkling back at me.

Not some roaring gaseous Kraken,

terrorising the seas of black.

But a reflection of the self,

smiling back at me.

I see you too, up there on that

purest pitch canvas.

For we are all stars.

Particles of exploded beasts,

rend millions of miles away,

and amalgamated into this.

Our bodies.

And a part of that star still shines in all of us.

In our sentience, our consciousness and our reason.

Some read the sacred scrolls to find answers.

Some seek the solace of a divinity divided from themselves.

But if you wish to find an answer,

look inside you.

You are creation.

You are the miracle.

Heaven exists within you,

and nowhere else.

Chapter 2 – WORK HARDER!

You get this one don't you? "Oh, haven't succeeded yet...then you're not working hard enough!" Well, smartarse, quite how do you know? Unless you're admitting to some kind of criminal stalking of my life don't you dare judge me or my efforts. Maybe you can't work hard enough on achieving your life dreams and goals; that's fine. Life has a funny way of putting things in our path that distract us: Relationships, family, misfortunes and regular everyday financial struggles. Any of these things in any combination could mean that you don't have the resources, either in terms of time or finance to chase your dreams as vehemently as you would like. But that does not make you a bad person. The success story types who like to produce tomes of their successes and impart their 'wisdom' to you will often fail to mention the fact that they are vacuous moral wastelands, veritable singularities of goodness, rending anything compassionate unto the void in order to achieve what they want. They leave out the parts where they left their wife/husband and kids to pursue their dreams, or spent time jetsetting around the world having extra-marital affairs with prostitutes. They will mention how they love their children so much they gave them the finest education but will leave out the fact that they spend hardly any time with their families because they are always too busy chasings dollars and dreams and then, in the ultimate insult, they will criticise you for not doing the same!

Don't believe it. Most people work more than hard enough to deserve to achieve their wildest ambitions; it is just that in this cut-throat world where money means more than humanity, your efforts are not appreciated by most. But I appreciate them. And I respect you for them. And I think the individual who puts their entire life's dreams on hold to do something nice for their fellow human being; to provide, to live, to love. They are the truly rich people, and they are the world's success stories.

It is a horrible world we live in where every minute of our time, professionally speaking, must be accounted for; where individuals must take time out of their holiday allowance to attend the funerals of loved ones because their companies and corporations do not understand compassion. My mother recently had a struggle with breast cancer, and it damn near crippled her financially and emotionally. She often had to fight tooth and nail with her employer to get paid time off for appointments, operations, recovery time and all sorts of other things that, disgustingly, should never have had questions asked about them. Luckily she had good friends in her Human Resources department to fight for her, but even this did not save her from the evils of the modern world, as complications following the removal of the tumour led to her having an infection that meant she had to have a further month off work UNPAID! Further complications still, following another operation resulted in her having to time recovery time off as holiday. And she has worked for the company in question for a quarter of a century, with little time off and plenty of overtime. For a period of about a year she worked 9am-11pm for the company due to their being busy, and her being an integral member of staff. She is always willing to cover for people who are ill or sick, whilst still doing her job to her fully ability. And yet, when circumstances led to her being ill, her company did not provide. And some would accuse her of not working hard enough!? Those people are disgusting, inhuman, uncompassionate scum. And humanity and compassion provides riches beyond the scope of any financial success. "Not working hard enough!" What a load of presumptuous, insulting, bollocks.

So don't ever let anyone make you believe you are not working hard enough. They are jealous. They are jealous because you have found a balance that means you can retain your humanity. They envy your ability to juggle so much at one time without falling over flat while they can only manage to do nothing but work, work, work and go home to copious consolation via the medium of grotesque amounts of red wine and masturbation. You deserve everything you have ever wished for and the only reason you do not have it is through blind, unpredictable fortune and your own commitment to not selling your fellow human being, your family, your friends, your compassion, indeed your very soul, down the river to get it. That is its own reward. There is no price that can be put on human compassion; there is no money in the world sufficient to pay for a human soul though some dare try to buy them. Don't let them, keep yours. Don't work harder, live more. Work is the consumption of a human being's humanity and it's transference into little more than cash via medium of labour. The less of that you do, the better. Spend time with your family and friends instead of staying behind to catch up at the office. Engage with your fellow human being by having a casual chat in a comfortable location and not an efficiency meeting in the boardroom. Be human, not automaton.

Solitary Soldier

Each step soothes
flitting over reflected sodium vapours.
Glistening gilt.
The streets only truly paved with gold
when the rain dances in a fluid mirror.

Damp hair drips
tickling, trickling down my poker face.
Stoic, unmoved.
Savouring every delicate kiss of cold
on blushing skin, from heaven's tears.

A warm squelch.
Peals from musical footwear.
Soggy sounds.
They seem to most discomforting.
To I like a pompous fanfare.

No other soul.
Abandoned pathways with no destination.
curve endlessly.
And I shall traipse every step of Earth.
For this Kingdom is mine.

Solitary soldier.

Marching alone, his only war

struggle internal.

And yet here I am the victor.

On sodden streets. Alone.

Chapter 3 – VISUALISE!

This is something these self-help gurus love to tout. Essentially, pretend, in your head, that it will go okay...and it will go okay! Act out your success in your head and your wildest dreams will come true! Oh how marvellous! I shall just sit about pretending that one day all self-help bastards will disappear off the face of the planet in some cataclysmic cosmic event, and one day THEY WILL!

To be fair, I'd love to slate visualisation but, actually, it is a useful tool. But these smarmy idiots will always tell you to make an effort to do it. This is nonsense. If you have to make an effort to visualise you achieving something then you probably should not be doing it in the first place! Sometimes situations will come up where you may have to do things you do not like interviews, presentations and meetings. These are good situations to force visualisation. But when it comes to achieving your life's goals, you should be imagining them every time your brain is not otherwise engaged. You should always be pondering what could happen, what should happen, what might happen, what happened last time; you should be thinking it all; because those dreams are yours. If you have to force it, you don't truly want it, and should spend your time thinking about those things you do want instead. Why, for example, waste time visualising what to say at a performance meeting for work, when you could be investing that time visualising things you can do to help friends and relatives? Why visualise for something you care not one jot about when you could be visualising about things you truly have a passion for? Visualisation in these self-help novels is little more than a positivity inducing (and vomit inducing!) exercise in self-delusion. It is a further way to make you think less like a human being and more like a robot. Compute what you should do, program yourself accordingly, and then do it. What of spontaneity? What of ability? What of truth and honesty? Why visualise lies to get yourself ahead when you could speak truths that may stunt you but are what your soul truly believes? Always be true to yourself, this is a key to happiness. Do not visualise so that you may think like they want you to think, or say what they want to hear. Visualise so that you may have faith and conviction in your own beliefs, in your own thoughts. You are a human being, thus you are entitled to your own thoughts, feelings and opinions, and your convictions in them shall be a much larger determination in your success in life than your desire to wish to sycophantically please others who deserve nothing from you but your honesty. Visualise yourself as a good human being and act accordingly and you shall have all the riches in the world; they may not be monetary, but they cannot be bought.

Your Eyes

Pearly White
With jewelled centre
Through which
Rays of light can enter.
They say
A window to the soul.
I say a cliché, bored and old.

An eye serves but one vital purpose
Ignored by poets rumbling murmurs.

It sees.
You deduce the rest.

Stay Thy Tongue

Stay thy tongue, offensive toad,
We like not what thou dost say.
From forked tongue comes a verbose load
of words for which thou shalt pay.

Hear not we the satire,
nor the unrelenting sadness
as thy mocking words expose a world
embracing serious madness.
Hear we thought naught critical
of existing perception,
aye, stay thy tongue, oh merciless devil;
in silence, no exception.

Ladies, Gentlemen, I do beseech,
grant this devil one more speech.
Is a word, and its reception
not the manifest of thy perception?
My tongue is neither bullet nor blade,
why then dost thou call it stayed?
Why, men may wound and mar and maim,

but I the one who takes the blame?
For choosing as my only sword
the harmless, sarcastic, spoken word?
A debate may be an ire, or bore
but preferable is that to war.
If all we did was speak our minds
for battle there would be no time.
For actions louder than words do speak
and actions, not words make futures bleak.
A battle of wits requires not strong arms,
but stronger minds, and much less harm.
And offense to words can be entombed
in ignorance; the same not true for wounds.
So I'll stay my tongue, aye, I'll cut it out.
And see how thou dost cope without
the chance for debate via reason and thought
or satire nonsensical and fool's words wrought.
An equal footing between offender and offended,
shall die when my flapping tongue be mended.
Instead, you'll replace my words with violence.
Aye, I'd take loud offense, over silence.

Chapter 4 – Believe in yourself.

Don't ever misinterpret this one. Self-help books about success do not mean 'believe in yourself' as a human entity, as I am proposing; but to believe in yourself as an individual. Believe in your own opinions as if you cannot possibly be wrong. Believe in your own actions as if they can never be wrong. This is stupid. This is stupid because you are human, you are flawed and you are not perfect. Blind, individualistic belief is a terrible thing, and a thought that is ruining humanity. Criticism is essential, and being able to accept it with objectivity is a very important quality. Having too much belief in what you are doing will only make you feel offended by criticism, rather than use it as a basis upon which to improve. This very notion of belief in individualism is what has allowed the steamrolling of human compassion and community for the sake of pursuit of individualistic wealth and success. Indeed, the best advice is not to believe in yourself but to believe in others. Have faith in, and respect for the people around you, even if they are saying things you might not like, because there is no success without others. What is the purpose of having the best job title, the biggest bank balance, and all the respect in the world if you go to a lonely home at night? What is the use in striving to achieve the world when you have no one to share it with? What is the point of blindly pursuing your own agenda if you alienate your friends and family in the process? There is none. Humanity is all one big family and rather than pursuing our own agendas as we are in some people's opinions entitled, we should always consider how it impacts on others around us; even if they are strangers.

Look, I don't mean this meanly. I am not suggesting your dreams and ideas are not important, indeed they are vital for you. But as discussed before, they are not always practical to achieve, and in your pursuit of them you could upset other people. You have to wonder whether such individual passions could truly make you happy if those important people around you are pushed away as a result of your trying. At the end of the day, you are not as important as you would like to think you are; again, I don't mean that in a mean way. But a human individual is totally insignificant. 1 in over 7,000,000,000 – There is nothing you could do that another probably could not do better given half a chance. But that insignificance, far from being a human weakness, is one of our greatest strengths as it should provide clarity, and perspective. What is truly important? You sealing your promotion, getting a job that has you travelling all over, and having to abandon your loved ones for long periods of time, while you expend your energy and soul in pursuit of further successes? Or doing less so that you can spend more time with the others around you; for they are truly important. Mortality is also an important thing to consider here, I know many do not wish to think about it, but it, too, provides great clarity and perspective. Would you rather die a financially poor individual surrounded by loved ones, or a successful rich individual dying alone? And when all is done, and you do finally snuff it, say there is an afterlife – I'm not suggesting there is, but merely for consideration's sake – say there is an afterlife. Are you going to be looking down on Earth from Heaven (again, assuming that's where you go! You could be a murderer for all I know, you may be heading straight to hell! This is just for an example, run with it) do you want to look down from heaven and say "Yeah, I'm dead now but, hell I made a lot of money while I was alive!" Or would you rather look down and observe the lives you've touched, the successes and happiness you made for others, the impact you had on humanity and not business? Our time on this Earth is all too fleeting and we have sadly been nurtured with a skewed idea as to what is actually important. It is saddening but it also provides opportunity, to learn the reality of things, to obtain true perspective on what is important in life. Belief in the self as an ego, this individualistic pursuit of what you want as important, this is truly dangerous. Belief in yourself as a human being, as a potential impact on others lives, as a fleeting bundle of cells and feelings, yet with the capacity to do many positive things for others, that is truly great.

To Dream

"To sleep, perchance to dream."
But, I desire not the heady
flights of fancy in my unconciousness.

When a nightmare strikes me
I want it to be conscious.
My sentience quivering in fear
as adrenaline clutches at my
rapidly thumping heart
pulling it into the dank,
murderous arched alleyway
of my throat.
Nightmares stalk the Earth during day,
and to feel them,
to know them,
one can fight them.
Lying prone and peaceful
none should fear.

And my dreams,
the colourful butterfly wishes
of love.
They are useless when at rest.
I want to feel the wellspring of joy

burst forth from my dilated,

glassy eyes.

I want every kind thought,

and idealistic hope to warm

the cold, depressing body of reality.

I want to be aware of the flight

of my soul through the pages

of imagined fantasy.

To dream in day is to change the world.

To lay prone and peaceful

one can change nothing.

And so, to sleep, perchance not to dream.

But to rest in the peaceful arms

of existential emptiness.

To swim static in the abyssal sea of naught

As my mind feasts gluttonously on the rest.

And prepares itself

to feel, to fear, to love, to hope.

To ensure my body is ready

to fight the vicious, cruel nightmares

and instigating idealistic, rainbow dreams.

Starlit Path

Inconsequential crystal flowers shattered at the touch
and a dust cloud formed in spectral tonalities;
Brownian motion, flitting, fleeting.
Gazing, stepping in the abyss
on a starlit path to nowhere.

Vast planets joined in matrimony, wed by ethereal rings
surrounded by icy, rocky crowds; their spectators.
A hole erupted in celebration, in unity and singularity
all were drawn into his magnetic abyss
on a starlit path to nowhere.

The tears of Shiva collided with sorry astral spirits
whose decay met with the wishful kiss of God
and the particles conjoined anew to form a cheeky smile.
The cradle of heaven's creation is an abyss
on a starlit path to nowhere.

Green leaves in the eyes of Man were stronger than the cosmos.
Guiding his hand to sin and misery unheard of, unseen,
unspoken.
Oh how he forgets that once suckled upon the teat of her,
his mother; from the womb of the abyss
on a starlit path to nowhere.

And thence were ideas lost and gone, with minds but a lingering memory
of the superconsciousness that exists in unity.
Everything is naught and naught everything.
For all is but the abyss
on a starlit path to nowhere.

Chapter 5 – Be Opportunistic!

Make and take your opportunities! That is what they say. Hell got a family funeral at the same time as an important job interview...pfft! What's grief to opportunity! Take the opportunity and forget the fact that other people might be in need of you. Because you are most important, right!? Piss off. I can't stand this kind of opportunistic thinking. Yes, we should all take opportunities when they come along, but only where they are practical and do not negatively impact others, and consequently, ourselves.

One phrase I cannot stand is "When life gives you lemons...Make lemonade!" I've always said "When life gives you lemons, fuck lemonade! Squirt lemon juice in life's eye, kick it in the genitals and show it who is actually in charge!" Make lemonade, what are you fucking crazy? Let's expand the metaphor; the lemon in your life is that your father has just died. Where the fuck is the lemonade in that? Unless you're the kind of heartless, soulless, callous individualist who rubs their hands with glee at the potential of an inheritance there is no lemonade to be made. Just a shitty situation you have to deal with. What if your lemons are rape!? Should you be busy trying to heal the often irreparable wounds, mental and physical that have been so cruelly inflicted upon you, or should you be thinking of writing it into a script for a Lifetime movie? That 'life gives you lemons...' kind of opportunism is disgusting and completely neglects the fact that you are a human being, with feelings, and emotions. It neglects the fact that you are a member of an extended community of others who may be in need. And what people usually need is not some opportunistically produced glass of bullshit lemonade. Opportunities are lovely. When they come along at the right time, they should be grasped with both hands. But sometimes the time is not right, sometimes your humanity, your compassion, your responsibility to others shall, and indeed should, get in the way. As said previously, you are not nearly as important as you would like to think and you need to assess whether your idealistically chasing opportunity is going to harm others. If the answer is yes, do the decent thing; pass up an opportunity for love and compassion. It's the right thing to do, the human thing to do.

And as for this 'make your opportunities' nonsense...This is just another extension of the 'work harder!' advice. True, things do not merely place themselves in our laps often, and you do have to work a little at making things happen. But this advice of doing everything in your power to make things happen not only again ignores the most prominent factor in life's success, of luck, but also implies that your achievements are more valuable than your commitments. They are another extension of advice that neglects you are a human being in a wider community, and merely panders to your ego and individualism by stating your opportunities are more important than other peoples. Say you've got a comfortable job, but are looking to improve, you network, and a few friends of friends later you've got a role lined up that you're poorly qualified for, have no idea how to do it, but pays better and is more along the lines of what you want to do. Meanwhile there could be a human individual out there better qualified than you, with more experience than you, and who maybe, just maybe, has worked harder to deserve the job more than you? Should your handshake of a friend of a friend, should your sycophantic figurative blow-jobbing of this person really lead you to be more deserving? Of course not! "But it's a dog-eat-dog world!" you say with a callous, wry smile. To which I reply "Oh good, I shall gladly murder you horrifically and consume your flesh you selfish, egotistical cunt." This is a truly horrible and totally erroneous claim. Do not cite Darwinian evolutionary theory and 'survival of the fittest' as some kind of excuse for your selfishness and inhumanity. It may have escaped your notice but humanity has somehow found a way to break free from the shackles of naturalistic savagery, so let's not use it an excuse when it suits us, eh? It would not stand up in a court of law, after having beat another person to death, that "Well, I was just stronger! Survival of the fittest and all that, your honour!" Because mankind has escaped the primal nature and can think, can reason, can determine what is right and wrong, and stomping over others more deserving for your own selfish gains is wrong. Just because some callous individuals have not made it illegal in a court of law, like they did with murder, it does not mean your conscience and morality should consider it okay. Remember your humanity, and trust your compassion. Assess your needs only in relation to those of others. If you are less in need, pass up a golden opportunity, or forever have someone else's miserable blood on your hands.

The Human Paradox

I'm extraordinary in my mediocrity.

A unique member of a uniform species.

My only significance is my insignificance.

I exist and yet, I'm not really here.

My paradoxes are meaningful in their meaninglessness.

I am everything, and nothing.

I am pressed for time in eternity.

I was yesterday to be tomorrow's today.

I've walked a million streets and got nowhere.

I work hard to doing nothing.

I am soul incarnate.

I am,

and that's all I need to be.

Chapter 6 – Love yourself

"You can't love anyone if you don't love yourself." That's the advice, isn't it? Well it's the advice of a fucking narcissist! Humility is key to loving others, because while you love yourself you will always think yourself deserving of love and while you think yourself deserving of love you will resent those who do not love you. It is a vicious cycle. I'm not saying everyone should be a miserable goat like I am; you are entitled to be happy with who you are. But love yourself!? What is most shocking is this is predominantly a wisdom extracted from Buddhism, usually the most selfless of religions! And yet, this advice of 'love yourself' is so selfish and erroneous.

Time for another personal anecdote; I am a depressive, with massive self-esteem issues. I loathe myself. I see the negativity in everything I do, and I see no positivity. I see a million and one areas of failure, and never believe I have ever truly achieved or had a success. I do not love myself. But I am capable of loving others, and indeed, my lack of love for myself means I will sacrifice myself, in time, in body, in opportunity, in order to do for others. I see each and every other human being as more important than I. Does this make me happy...well sadly not, but I'm a depressive. If you aren't, and you see the impact it has on other people when you are there for them no matter what, when you sacrifice yourself to do right by them, you will be rich indeed. You will be loved. And love is a wealth unquantifiable. Do not love yourself; merely work hard to make others love you. A love from another is worth more than any self-congratulatory, onanistic love for yourself, by yourself.

I mean seriously, just think of it, "Love yourself" – It's a negative thing! It's a criticism we have of people "Oh, he loves himself!" we use it to denote narcissism, self-adoration, and undeserved self-praising individuals. So why then, in the same respect, do we propose it is impossible to love others without being a self-entitled narcissist? It goes against logic! As I said, I don't think everyone should loathe themselves as I do indeed self-respect and self-like are positive things. But self-love is too strong to ever be positive. It shall give you false senses of entitlement, it will make you resent those who do not feel the same about you, and you will hurt them because of it. You will be a spiteful individual. So please do not love yourself. Instead, invest your time in loving others, and showing them that you deserve to be loved in return by them. This is altogether a much more fruitful and compassionate use of what is one of the strongest of human feelings, and subsequently, rather than have to rely solely upon yourself for love, others will make sure you never want for it, just as you did they. Love others sparingly; love yourself little, that is my advice.

Share a Smile

There's always time to share a smile,
no matter what the time of day.
Fear not for petty ridicule;
Worry not what 'they' might say.
Do not hesitate to place
yourself at the bottom of the pile
if it puts a smile on another's face
then it is truly worth your while.
Even if it's half 3 in the morn,
and you are tired as hell,
spread love, and joy; not callous scorn.
If we all do this, the world is well.

Chapter 7 – In Summary

I can't tell you how to live your lives, that is for you and you alone. I can give my advice, my opinions, my beliefs and my thoughts, but I cannot give you orders. But we would do well to remember our humanity, in all that we do. We are all individuals, yes, but the same can be said of the cells in our bodies and, like human beings, they do not cope too well on their own either. We are at our strongest, our richest and our most successful when we are at our most unified.

What is more, we are always told to desire and covet the big things. We want the biggest, most palatial houses, the best cars, and the most wealth. But how much joy do these things bring us? Take comfort in the little things, the minutiae of life are the most wonderful joys. How much more joy can you get from a meal that costs you a fortune that you do not get from sharing a cheap ice cream on a lovely day with your family or friends? Why seek the joy of the fastest, most expensive car when a short walk can often be the most rewarding and joyous mode of transport?

But most of all, love. Love everything but yourself (see the chapter above for thoughts on that.) To truly love you shall be blessed with riches beyond your imaginings because with love comes appreciation, and respect. Love can help you stop draining yourself, physically and mentally, pursuing what you don't really want or need, and focus instead on that and those which you do. Love can stop you chasing stars, and allow you to be one. And I don't mean love in the horrid, vain, materialistic, narcissistic and unrealistic portrayal of it in most fiction and films. Forget that fairytale. Love goes beyond what a man and a woman get up to with the lights turned off. Love is not something to be given and taken; it is something that should be as ever-present as atmospheric gases! It should float in the ether around us all, being emitted by all, and possessed by none. Love is not hanging around in bars chasing skirt. Love is not speed-dating on some dreary, wet, Tuesday evening. Love is, to this day, despite millennia of evolution in mankind's thought and philosophy, still indescribable, immeasurable, unquantifiable, elusive and yet, treasured. Love is worth more than all the money in this sorry, greedy world. Love is life.

Your Unicorn is Just a Horse

One day you must just close the book
and tell yourself
"The fairytale does not exist."

The melancholy shall pass.
You will learn the hollow futility
of mourning the loss
of something you never even had
to lose.

Your eyes, strained and teary
will, for a while,
see only shades of sad blue-grey.
But colour will return.
Vibrancy will come again.

And as you see the world anew

you will spy new opportunities.

New tales, greater than those fictions.

You will see that your unicorn

is just a horse.

But with it you can do many a great thing.

And the truth. That provides great clarity.

In this tale

even the good guys die in the end.

The Theory of Relativity V. 2.0 – Love

Bound by laws we pontificate.
Scientists day by day try to figure them out.
Hypothesis and theory abounds, but, no answer.

Religion tries to find the right ones yet,
division leads to their questioning.
They do not have it right; no answer.

Everyday people usually wander
aimlessly, bound by the rules but un-fussed.

But each emerald pasture,
or delicate, virgin tundric snowfield;
Each rolling ocean, crashing percussive
against time long, always strong cliffs;
They know the answer.

The cosmos has myriad rules binding
her processes. Like clockwork they work
regular, precise, balanced.

If enough scientists and mathematicians
could put their dogmas aside
and word hard, they would see.
All are one.
There is but one overriding rule.
LOVE=Everything.
Love is the answer to all your questions.

There is nothing sweeter, greater or more powerful.
Love=Everything.

Love can hit you faster than the speed of light.
It can make you leap as though gravity does not exist.
It can overbear your natural instincts.
Love is the most powerful force in the universe.
So let's use it.
I love you.

Chapter 8 – It's About Time!

Time, it is a universal binding to all, given how all is finite. And yet we have a habit of using it so unwisely. What does our society deem we do with our time? Encourage and embrace the ingeniousness and creativity of the human mind and body? Perform selfless acts of love and compassion on our fellow human beings? Indulge in thought for thought's sake, simply because expanding one's mind is a wonderful thing? Nope, none of the above! Instead, perform remedial task for money, lather, rinse and repeat. How horrific, how shameful, that mankind should be treated thus. As little more than capital tied up in labour and sealed by time. Time is so infinitely valuable, so priceless and yet our governments and our businesses would dare have the nerve to place a price tag on it, and we, being the generally passive and accepting people we are, allow them to do so.

These self-help guides will always tell you the importance of time management. You must be efficient they say, and prioritise. But just what should your priorities be? How can you claim a shift or a meeting or an interview is more important than investing your time in yourself and your loved ones? Where is the humanity in that? There quite simply is none. A human being need worry nothing of time, beyond what best to do for others with the short period of it we are given as life. And yet we must sell it. Our entire economy is built around the notion of selling your time on this Earth to someone else. It is truly saddening, the lack of humanity and compassion in it. The lack of respect for an individual's life, that their time is worth nothing until they are selling it to you! And this idea that those who indulge in thought and daydreaming are in some way 'wasting time' – I beg to differ! The pursuit of thought is a far better use of a human being's time than performing repetitive tasks for something as base and worthless as money. Money is infinite, in that it is merely a conceptual idea used to promote trade of goods, and, those who are vulgar enough that they print it can make as much as they want, your time, however, is finite and that makes it worth so much more than the meagre price tag placed upon it.

Moments

This right here.
That is now history.
This is now.
No, it's history too.
What about now? Is now now?
Nope, sorry, now has been and gone.
Passed into past.
What was now is now then.
Well what about now then?
Nope, past too.
Well when will now be now!?
Soon
How soon!?
Now
Now!?
No, just then.

Each tick the clock's hand slaps the face of the present
sending it flying back into the past.
And with its other hand, ushers in the future
proclaims it the King of now with a crown of cloud
and as fast as the future arrives, its crown evaporates
and it's slapped into history.

The fractal spiral of time is too confusing for me.
Washing over us like a backwards river
swelling tides of events flow from the ocean of potential
to the minute tributaries and springs of recorded past.
While man marks it with arbitrary meter.
There is no time. What was has gone, what is is going and what will will go.
All we have is now.
Now?
No now!
Just then?
Fuck it.
Smash your watch,
turn off the alarm,
delete the clock function on your phone
put a square over the time on your computer screen
and if they put a clock on your TV switch it off.
Now is now and it's all we have.
And all we'll ever have.
Don't worry about then.
Don't plan for soon.
Just be now.

When?
SHUT UP!

Moments Part II - Conversational Time Travel

Time's knife slices lines of longitude
and darkness and light creep around
following them and enforcing their rule;
The sun and moon but night-watchmen
of Time's tyrannical regime.

Communications across these lines
are like conversational time travel.
Discovering tomorrow's occurrences today.
Happenings now that occurred tomorrow
yet are happening in someone's yesterday.

It all merely exists to highlight Time
and its consistent inconsistency.
Whether shortest moment,
or longest eternity
it matters not;
because they don't exist.

There is no today, tomorrow, or yesterday
but in our minds and memories.

All there is, is now, and now has just gone
as it always shall go just as you realise it.

Chapter 9 – And now for something completely different...

Well, I've bored you enough with my cosmic-hippy, humanitarian bullshit philosophies already, so, here I am going to be sharing a small collection of some of my more positive poems. Why? Do they fit in with the theme of this book? Well, some maybe, some may not. But they fit in with one of themes and that is remembering to appreciate the little things. Some of these are about matters as trivial as nommy foodstuffs, one is a nostalgic look back at what could have been, and why, because it wasn't, it is so beautiful, and one is a piece of nonsense about a lemur. Either way, there are here in the hope that they provide some joy, or some thought. I would have liked to have written chapters in my satirical self-help tome to provide them a suitable and appropriate home, but how does one include a chapter on the simple beauty of the blush of a lady. Or the nostalgic joy of school crushes, and indeed, how does one write a chapter in a satirical self-help tome about a lemur on one's femur!? So they have their place here, as the epilogue, to remind you never to take anything too seriously, for it is all too fleeting, too precious, too beautiful and too damn funny! Life is the greatest comedy we shall ever see. Embrace it.

Blushing

What cosmic sweet nothings are whispered,
softly, and lovingly into the ears of the sky
to make it blush such a rich magenta
as the sun rises and falls?

What words of love,
or delicate, yet unsuspected kiss
does the sun bestow upon her
that she should turn such shade?

Aye, but a blushing sky is only half as magnificent
as the delicate rose hued cheeks of a lady;
her coy smile setting her face in a pose
as timeless and pulchritudinous
as pre-Raphaelite oil on canvas.

How I long to brush those rouged cheeks
with my rude, unworthy hand.
How much I want to embrace that timeless beauty
and absorb the warmth emanating from her soul
and ease the freezing of my own shattered icicle heart
So that I, like the sky, may feel kissed by the sun.
And hear those same words that make our cerulean canopy
turn pink, and flushed with arousal.

The Lemur

I walked around for six months with a lemur on my femur
and it professed to me that it's job was as a hotel cleaner,
and I must admit I was confused, to me it didn't seem a
lemur on my femur could ever be a cleaner.
But I was a dreamer, so the lemur on my femur
I agreed must be a cleaner, and I must surely deem a
cleaner lemur on my femur to be a great poetic theme, a
truly silly poem that would match the lemur's demeanour.

Now the cleaner lemur on my femur was adept at hopping
and hopping never stopping I set it off to do my shopping.
To his iPod bobbing, to the latest hits chart topping
the cleaner lemur on my femur set off to do my shopping.
But clumsy was the lemur so my bags he kept on dropping
and the whopping mass of products in their packaging were popping
and soaked with sweat and sopping, the lemur stopping hopping
and his gait took on a dejected form, a-limping and a-lopping.
And thus it was with sadness that the lemur needed chopping.

So the cleaner lemur on my femur was, quite rightly sacked
and the clothes he had unpacked were duly restacked and
repacked.
But the lemur, I, he tracked until my rota he could enact
and catching me quite unawares, I was, in fact, attacked.
The lemur smacked and whacked upon my intestinal tract
and trying to escape I found my feet, they had been tacked
unto the floor in measures merely to distract,
as the cleaner lemur, from my femur, my computer hacked!
I feared my attention slacked, this plot I'd failed to react
with sufficient haste to prevent my life being ransacked.
My identity he cracked and took it as his own, in fact,
as business in my name the lemur began to transact.
Now he, the cleaner lemur, my curse, my anathema
was I, the human dreamer and I
The cleaner lemur who did dwell upon my femur.

Hand-Me-Downs

He stood by the counter a raggamuffin in a rag-tag of rags.
A young boy in too-big-for-his-feet hand me down shoes.
His hand me down jeans loose on his hips
covered by the hem of a filthy, hand me down shirt.
He hands over his hand me down wealth
a plethora of coin that has burned holes in history's pockets.
The store keeper hands the boy down a dream,
and hands him back his hand me down cash.

"A dream is free." said the clerk.
The hand me down frown of the boy turned around,
into a smile, a hand me down smile, given by the clerk.

Cookies

The delicate speckled surface
craggy and lunar in appearance.
Like a tiny, tasty moon,
just for you.
Each pitted crater holds
an extraterrestrial treasure;
a small, warm cocoa comet,
denting the lunar landscape.
And as each morsel
trundles along its orbit
into the gaping, black-hole,
you will savour the dream.
Even after it has gone,
it will stay with you.
"But why does it have to go?"
You ask.
Because that's just the way
the cookie crumbles.

The Shadow

I am a shadow. Ever present,
Humanoid in form and shape,
extant only when there is no light,
yet I have no soul.
I have no voice to speak
yet I am louder than you.
You can try and shake my hand
but yours shall pass through mine.
I have no time for petty shows of respect.
I mirror your thoughts, your actions,
so that when negativity occurs,
you blame yourself.
While you stand in the hot glare
of the bright lights,
I am behind you, shaded, shielded.
You work hard, and I mimic you
but I do nothing. I need do nothing.
You will do it for me.
I am your shadow.
You cannot get rid of me.

Ah! But I can.
You are my shadow,
and to purge myself of you
I need only surround myself
in light. From all angles.
Enlightenment will slay
the shadow.

Cliff Seed

You opened them up, your arms
like the petals of a beautiful flower
basking in the sun.
You created energy from nothing
but her bounteous rays
and your own resourcefulness.
While I, on craggy cliff top clung
in dusty, barren soil
ever reaching for the sun
from which an outcrop shaded.

Your arms could be my nursery,
in which to plant root
and germinate.
We could share the sun,
we could share warmth,
and we could share life;
Existence in symbiosis.

But, alas, your flower
is too large and beautiful a bloom
for me to deserve it.
You shall always, like radar-head
of a sunflower, aim yourself at the sun,
While I shall always seek shade.
You shall always be the prettier;
you shall always get the attention.
While I, weed like, creeping and clinging
like ivy to your good fortunes.

Nature smiled not on me
when she sowed my seed.
And so, I shall forego our symbiosis.
I shall allow you to bloom free
and beautiful, away from my
leeching tendrils.
And I shall struggle on.
On this cliff top.
In shade.
And one day I shall go from
a struggling sprout
to a looming, majestic tree.
And your flower shall be welcomed
'neath my canopy.

Ice Cream

Delicate crystals twinkle,
formed into a ball and placed
atop a waffled king
like some sweet, majestic crown.

Each molten drip that falls
down the sides of the crispy
body that holds it aloft,
looking like creamy tears of joy.

And each lap a labour of love
as you savour the sweet creamy flavour.
Ice cold, yet so warming.
A sweet treat, a delight in heat.

It's About Fucking

Two vines intertwined
a verdant mesh and mangle.
Dripping dew drops
the malachite lovers entangled
in unbridled glory.

Nature holds no greater beauty.
As one viridian beast locks with another,
fairer in texture, in heart, in spirit
and clasps his myriad tendrils around her
prickling at her delicate stoma
with his proud, erect thorns.

A savagely beautiful act,
from which flowers bloom
and sweet fruits grow;
and seeds of progeny planted
make the miracle of life.

On Rolling Stock

On rolling stock
Sat mirthing rabble.
Chuckling, grinning
Geese; a gaggle.

Cackling witches;
Perms and hairspray
Not a word I think they daren't say.
Hairdryers, highlights, husbands
Dongs, dirt, desires and dildos.

Filthy tarts, their laughter chronic
Have another gin and tonic.

A wry smile becomes this face of mine
When youth get blamed for moral decline.

The Battle of Earth and Tide

A masterful painter has,
on pale cerulean canvas
with pink tinted bands,
brushed wisps of pure white.
In the corner of this
wondrous watercolour
clings the form of a dazzling
opalescent spectre.
His desperate, shimmering tears
rebounding off the freeform,
glassy surface below.
Their angelic ghosts dancing
in the darkness.

The airborne spectral opal
wills the seemingly endless seas
unto land's cushioning bed.

A pebble; so small, so insignificant

erodes gradually in the face of

the oceanic onslaught.

But the pebble is not alone.

Arm in arm she stands

with her brothers and sisters.

Siblings uniform, stoically resist

against the raging, torrential war

of tide.

Alone, insignificant.

Together, unstoppable. Immovable.

All pebble shall, one day,

be worn to sand.

But new rocks shall form.

New pebbles shall be

and Gaia's unbroken spirit

shall never be

shattered to sand

by the unending sea.

Chalk Dust Memories

Ballpoint scrawled desks
etched with idealistic youthful wisdoms
and hallowed bikeshed conversations
carried on the wind like fallen leaves;
drowned out only by the dull thud
of footballs on old, red brick.

KM heart SB IDST
and similar promises of love everlasting
Tip-Exxed on lockers
and secured in place by numbered keys;
that imprison so many secret,
fleeting
playground romances.

And yet I never told her how I felt.
I never asked "Will you go out with me?"
My heart was my locker.
And I allowed the years to slip by
like the small, grubby bits
that come off an eraser.

Maybe a ruler could have helped me to see straight?

And stopped me running around

and around

Like a compass

in protracted circles in my head.

That Bunsen burning in my soul was all for you

and, had I the power of English to express myself.

Were I able to do the mathematics

and put 2 and 2 together.

Had I known for sure the Chemistry between you and I.

Maybe my History books would have read different.

But; I am glad.

Because when the bell sounds for me

and my day comes to an end.

Home time.

I can lay in dreams and see your visage.

My secret school crush; an unblemished ideal.

Wandering through the hazy snow

of halcyon chalk dust memories.

I Declare World Peace

As the golden flower blooms
and spreads its petals wide
over the dividing line
between Earth and Heaven.
I declare world peace.

As sleepy digits caress
the remains of last night's
peaceful illusion
from weepy, weary eyes,
I declare world peace.

As suds smooch the steamy air
and enamel receives bristled kisses;
a loving cleansing
harmonious atmosphere,
I declare world peace.

While donning nature's gift
of woven plant and earth,
a figurative fig leaf
Covering man's modesty,
I declare world peace

With each lamb-like cautious step
and inhale and exhale of invisible
soul nourishment,
and each minute,
I declare world peace.

The golden flower, tucked up, tired,
paints the sky the softest tones.
With this warm, pink hued hug,
basking in nature's bosom.
I declare world peace.

Glistening firefly fancies aflame
against inviting endless void.
A journey starts, I depart
and alight at dreams in which
I declare world peace.

Chapter 10 – And Finally

What follows is a transcript of tweets I made on twitter on September 16th 2011 – The day prior to the beginning of the Occupy Wall Street action in New York. My entire basis for support of this movement is laid out in the previous chapters and I wish to share my tweets from that day as they express and sum up many of the things written above in a much more concise fashion. I also quote Bob Marley quite a bit thanks to his being prominent on my playlist at the time, but there is nothing wrong with quoting Bob! It does sound more than a little crazy at times but I was rather possessed by a spirit of love that, truly, I cannot explain. I literally do not remember my writing these words, and their existence is only known due to my having saved them! Either way, these are my closing statements, my rallying cry to humanity to be more human. My rallying cry in a world of fear and hate to love more. True success, true wealth, it cannot be measured by any but yourself. It is not your job role or your tax contributions. It is not your bank balance, nor your level of responsibility. True success comes from doing what is right as a human being, and true wealth is the love you receive for doing so. They mean more than any vain, superficial success in the realms of business and money.

Thank you for reading.

Karl Mercer.
Peace and love. X

Love is the Only Currency I Recognise

Love is the only currency I recognise. Sadly Governments and banks don't deal in it. This is why #IWillOccupy
No Woman, No Cry. This is #whyweoccupy. Oh my little darling, don't shed no tears.
The tears of another human being have a value all the banks in the world could not pay. The struggle of another life has no pricetag.
We are all one in humanity and I say it's time we stopped checking on our bank balances and started checking on our neighbours.
I say it's time we give up competing against our brothers and sisters and work together for each other. Drop the competition myth.
Fear for your fellow human being is manufactured. Fear should be replaced with love. Because life is too short and precious.
They say the world is getting smaller. This is why they have to manufacture fear. They are scared we will realise the oneness of humanity.
They are scared that it doesn't matter what your background, skin colour, religion or creed is. We are all one.
We are stardust. Particles blown into a universal bubble in an infinite expanse. We are all the same. We are one with the Earth

and sky too.

Life is an illusion. Life is a cosmic sneeze. An outburst of energy that created this, most miraculous time and day.

And you are the biggest miracle of all. A collective of particles with the potential to see and understand, to think.

But your thoughts have been hijacked. People are manipulating your most base behaviours, so you have to utilise your most sophisticated ones.

As humans, we can do this. We can overcome our base desires to see the bigger picture. And the biggest picture of all is this…

…all is one, in everything; and nothing.

Let's be one. Let us come together in oneness, unity, peace, freedom and Love

And to you dirty, rotten bankers and politicians. I love you too. You're fools. You're ignorant. I pity you. But we must be cruel to be kind.

WOO Can you feel the cosmic love? I can feel it. I can feel the kiss of a distant star when the wind stings my skin with bitter cold.

I feel the magnificence of the universe with every delicate kiss from a raindrop. I inhale the vacuum void with every breath.

The money you hold in your hand is nothing but the same fragile dust as you and I.

One day money will return to dust just as we. But which would you like to go first?

some people like to diss religion. Don't. Love it. It holds the beautiful poetry of creation.

It holds every horrid lesson of history man should learn not to emulate and contains all the wise words of love man should follow.

Read them words. Study them, but study them without man's imposed dogma.

Study them with a free mind and a free heart and you shall find God and you will see that his/her name is LOVE.

Love is not from the movies. Love is not just a man and a woman getting sweaty (although that is awesome!)

Love's a state of mind. Love's a state of being. Love is still after tens of thousands of years of evolution and history still inexplicable.

ONE LOVE. ONE HEART. LET'S GET TOGETHER AND FEEL ALRIGHT (Bob, it's like you're soul is with me right now!)

Let's get together to fight this Holy Armageddon. It doesn't have to happen. We can be one. We can be together in unity not economy.

We can live in peace and unity of only we can make the 6billion other folks who feel just like us realise IT CAN HAPPEN.

There is nothing the human mind, heart, soul and LOVE cannot do. We can achieve anything. Why? Because we are. Because we exist.

We exist and that means that every modicum of this universe is in us. We own it. We control it.

Mother Earth cradles us, but we support her too. And we hold in our hands the whole universe.

And when you lay on your death bed you can crack a smile and say "I own this!" And you shall know you lived. You controlled. You loved.

I can feel it people. I can feel it on the wind. You can feel it in the Earth. It rumbles. More than ever, It calls us.

There's a natural mystic blowin' thru the air.

Some say Sept. 17th shall be a protest. I don't call it a protest. I call it a start. The first trumpet, before all Babylon falls.

Special Thanks

My deepest and sincerest thanks to you for purchasing this. In doing so, you are doing more than buying an eBook; you are helping a young individual achieve his personal dreams, and allowing him the freedom to assist others with theirs. You are truly a wonderful person, and I thank you, and I love you.

Printed in Great Britain
by Amazon.co.uk, Ltd.,
Marston Gate.